O is for

OBAMA

The Washington Post

Written by **Dana Milbank**   Illustrated and designed by **Mark Anderson**

Anyone who thinks that nothing ever changes in Washington is wrong. Everything changes in Washington, all the time—the issues, the obsessions, the players, the alliances, the grudges, the haircuts. The only constant, in fact, is the regularity of change. Every two years there will be a few new faces on Capitol Hill, both on the House and Senate sides. Every four or eight years there will be a new first family in the White House. Those of us who live here are accustomed to an ever-shifting landscape. Figuring out who's who and what's what is almost a routine exercise.

Usually, that is. Once in a great while, instead of predictable change we experience utter transformation. The election of Barack Obama was one of these political…well, pick your cliché: earthquakes or tsunamis or hundred-year floods. Whatever it was, it left Washington all but unrecognizable. Herewith, to help get our bearings, an alphabetical primer on the shape of our fair city in the Age of Obama.

Eugene Robinson, columnist and associate editor, The Washington Post

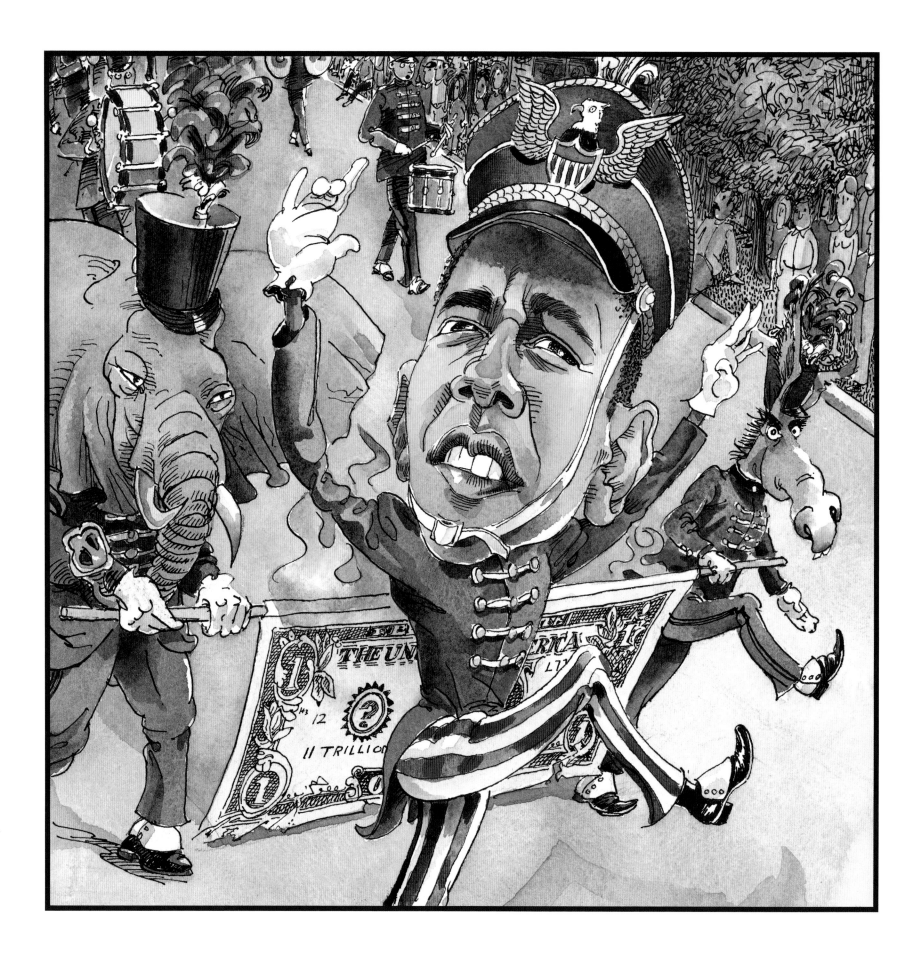

"A" is for

in economic trauma.

The nation is counting on

A skinny guy named Obama.

When President **BARACK** Obama took office in January 2009, the American economy was experiencing what many described as the worst downturn since the Great Depression. The nation had been in recession for 13 months, stock markets had fallen about 40 percent in 2008, and 2.6 million people had lost jobs. Obama pushed through Congress a stimulus package that he said would save or create 3.5 million jobs, but job losses continued at first and the package swelled the forecasted federal deficit.

"B" is for

BIDEN,

Always good for a laugh.

He opens his mouth...

And out pops a gaffe.

VICE PRESIDENT Joe Biden is famous for what Obama calls "rhetorical flourishes." During the campaign, he declared that Senator Hillary Clinton was "more qualified than I am to be vice president," told a supporter in a wheelchair at a rally to "Stand up—let the people see you," and declared that FDR was president during the 1929 stock market crash and "got on television"— a technology that was not yet in commercial use. After becoming vice president, Biden referred to an Internet address as a "website number," and the White House had to issue a correction after he advised people not to travel by airplane during the swine flu outbreak.

"C" is for

A survivor first-rate.

Just when you thought she was finished,

Voilà! Secretary of state!

After the humiliation of her husband, President Bill Clinton's impeachment in connection with a sex scandal involving a White House intern, Hillary Clinton recovered and won a Senate seat representing New York. She was the prohibitive favorite to win the Democratic presidential nomination in 2008 but was upended by the long-shot campaign of Barack Obama. She seemed destined to limp back to the Senate without even a committee chairmanship until Obama, who famously dismissed Clinton as "likable enough" during their bitter presidential primary battle, made the surprise choice to name her the nation's top diplomat.

"D" is for  DRUDGE,

Who, like LIMBAUGH and HANNITY,
Believes that Obama
Is causing calamity.

The **OBAMA** presidency has been a boon for the opposition media. Matt Drudge's online Drudge Report gets about 500 million page views a month, Rush Limbaugh's radio show gets about 20 million listeners a week, and Sean Hannity gets nearly 2.5 million viewers a night on Fox News. Limbaugh in particular has found his voice as a de facto opposition leader, saying he hopes Obama fails as president.

"E" is for ELEPHANT,

Republican pachyderm.
This species is endangered,
At least in the short term.

Following REBUBLICAN presidential nominee John McCain's lopsided loss to Obama in 2008, the GOP reached a historic low: only 21 percent of Americans identified themselves as Republicans in a Washington Post poll. The chief strategist for McCain's campaign called his party a "shrinking entity" and warned that it is "extinct" or "near extinct" in various parts of the country. But in politics, fortunes can change very quickly.

"F" is for

FANNIE,

Like AIG too big to fail.

First a bailout, then big bonuses;

For this nobody goes to jail?

THE FEDERAL GOVERNMENT'S various agencies coughed up about $400 billion to take over mortgage giants Fannie Mae and Freddie Mac and about $180 billion to rescue insurance behemoth American International Group—not to mention about $700 billion to shore up banks and other financial companies and tens of billions of dollars to shepherd Chrysler and General Motors through bankruptcy. Lawmakers were not amused when they learned that AIG had used some bailout money to pay bonuses.

"G" is for

GORE,

Who talks of Earth's demise.

He hasn't cooled us down yet,

But he won a Nobel Prize.

SINCE HIS LOSS in the disputed 2000 presidential election, former vice president Al Gore has made a fortune for himself and has become an international celebrity for his efforts to combat global warming. His various ventures and works, including his famous book and slide presentation-turned-documentary film, An Inconvenient Truth, have won him and his collaborators an Oscar, an Emmy, and even the Nobel Peace Prize.

"H" is for

Huffington,

A huge Obama fan.

Do others love him so much?

Maybe Maddow or Olbermann.

Greek-born Arianna Huffington, once married to a Republican congressman, converted from a conservative into a liberal activist and started the popular Huffington Post website. Her following is almost as passionate as that of Keith Olbermann and Rachel Maddow, liberal prime-time hosts on the MSNBC cable network. The three were harsh critics of George W. Bush but have largely defended the White House since Obama took office.

"I" is for

Run by some kooks.
This would be amusing
If they didn't make nukes.

PEACE!

From the lavish living of the shah to the anti-American fervor of the Ayatollah Khomeini, the rulers of Iran have long been a bit off-kilter. President Mahmoud Ahmadinejad continued the pattern, calling the Holocaust a "great deception," declaring that there are no gays in Iran, and trying to destabilize the U.S.-backed government in neighboring Iraq. Ominously, he continues to pursue technology that could allow him to develop a nuclear bomb—and though masses of Iranians protested Ahmadinejad's 2009 reelection, his opponent, Mir Hossein Mousavi, also wants nukes.

"J" is for the JUSTICES

On a court plagued by division.
They bicker, squabble, then release
Another 5-to-4 decision.

THE HIGH COURT has four reliably conservative justices and four generally liberal justices, with moderate Ronald Reagan appointee Anthony M. Kennedy often serving as the crucial fifth vote. As a result, recent cases on abortion, gun control, capital punishment, global warming, and terrorism have been decided by votes of 5 to 4. Only if one of the four conservatives departed would Obama be able to shift the balance.

"K" is for **KISS** and make up,

A gesture that's strictly token.

Every four years they pledge bipartisanship,

And within days the promise is broken.

It's CoMMON after an election for the winner to talk about "bipartisanship." Obama made a point early in his presidency to sit down with Republican lawmakers to get their thoughts. But he quickly observed that "old habits die hard," and Congress quickly returned to the party-line voting prevalent under George W. Bush—who had also pledged to set aside partisan differences but never achieved that goal. The Democratic majority in the House passed Obama's economic stimulus plan without a single Republican vote.

"L" is for

LOBBYISTS,

A capital institution.

Just pass the laws they want,

And you'll get a contribution.

IT HAS OFTEN BEEN SAID that the United States has the best government money can buy, and there's some truth to that. Despite round after round of lobbying and ethics reform—including efforts to clamp down after the Jack Abramoff scandal in which several lawmakers and government officials were convicted—lobbyists and lawmakers continue to find loopholes. In exchange for "earmarks"—pet projects inserted into spending bills—lobbyists help raise money to reelect lawmakers.

"M" is for Michelle,

**Whose tastes are quite fine.
At the White House she grows
Organic arugula and thyme.**

First Lady Michelle Obama has generally brought a common touch to the White House, eschewing high-fashion labels for off-the-rack clothes from the likes of J. Crew. But she showed a hint of elite tastes when she set out to grow an organic garden at the White House that would include arugula, the high-priced leafy vegetable that got her husband in trouble in 2007 when he asked an uncomprehending crowd in Iowa: "Anybody gone into Whole Foods lately and see what they charge for arugula?" (The natural-foods chain doesn't have stores in Iowa.)

"N" is for *Nuptials,*

Girl-girl and boy-boy.
It's cool in states like Vermont
But California sees no cause for joy.

By mid-2009, six states had decided to legalize same-sex marriage: Connecticut, Iowa, Maine, Massachusetts, New Hampshire, and Vermont. New York and Rhode Island, as well as the District of Columbia, recognized such unions from other states, while Hawaii, New Jersey, Oregon, and Washington had provisions to give unmarried couples some spousal benefits. But California voters approved, and the State Supreme Court upheld, a ballot initiative making same-sex marriage unconstitutional. The battle continues there and in several other states.

"O" is for **OBAMA**,

An impressive speech-giver.

Now the nation's waiting

To see if he'll deliver.

BARACK Obama's list of promises was long: restore economic growth, bail out Wall Street and the automakers, create millions of jobs, end the war in Iraq, defeat al-Qaeda, improve America's standing in the world, reverse global warming, overhaul the nation's health-care system, save the Social Security and Medicare programs, and balance the federal budget. "I think even our critics would agree that, at the very least, we've been busy," the president speculated after three months on the job. It remains to be seen whether his efforts will succeed. The voters will decide, on November 6, 2012.

"P" is for

PELOSI,

Madam speaker of the House.
Her strong-arm tactics are disguised
In a silk Armani blouse.

THE FIRST WOMAN to be speaker of the House is no shrinking violet. As Nancy Pelosi put it, "Anybody who's ever dealt with me knows not to mess with me." Of her opponents, she has said, "If people are ripping your face off, you have to rip their face off." She punishes those who defy her by denying them committee chairmanships, and she has even taken on the CIA, accusing agency operatives of lying when they briefed her about interrogation tactics.

"Q" is for al-Qaeda,

They've got us figured wrong.
We're free to laugh at our leaders,
Which shows why America is strong.

al-Qaeda doesn't know quite what to make of Obama, whom the terrorist group's leaders have derided as a "hypocrite," a "killer" of innocents, and an "enemy of Muslims." If they were hoping for a less confrontational American leader, Obama squashed that when he announced in Europe, "It is important for Europe to understand that even though I'm now president and George Bush is no longer president, al-Qaeda is still a threat, and that we cannot pretend somehow that because Barack Hussein Obama got elected as president, suddenly everything's going to be okay."

"R" is for RAHMBO,
White House staff chief.
If you dare cross him
You'll end up with grief.

RAHM EMANUEL, whom colleagues in the Clinton White House nicknamed "Rahmbo" after the Sylvester Stallone movie character Rambo, is known for his foul mouth and his take-no-prisoners style. He is alleged to have sent a rotten fish to a pollster who gave him bad advice. Obama joked of the former congressman: "Every week, the guy takes a little time away to give back to the community. Just last week, he was at a local school, teaching profanity to poor children."

"S" is for

specter,

Who thought switching parties was fun.

Democrats said: Welcome, Arlen!

Republicans said: Son of a gun!

During his 30 years in the Senate, Pennsylvania's Arlen Specter had been a moderate. But that got him into trouble with conservatives in the Republican Party, who were on the verge of beating him in a primary. So rather than accept almost certain defeat, an opportunistic Specter became a Democrat, giving his new party enough of a majority in most cases to overcome GOP filibusters. His former colleagues called him a turncoat, and the Republican Party chairman accused him of "flipping the bird" at GOP leaders.

"T" is for the
Treasury.

It's empty now–don't ask!
We had some money here somewhere,
But Tim Geithner lost it on TurboTax.

The federal debt now exceeds $11 trillion–with a "T." And the nation's deficit for fiscal 2009, projected to be in the vicinity of $2 trillion, shatters all records. The deficit, equivalent to 12.9 percent of gross domestic product, is the highest since World War II. The man keeping an eye on this, Treasury Secretary Tim Geithner, has enough trouble tracking his own finances. He apologized and paid the government $42,702 because of underpayments found in his personal tax returns, which he prepared using the software program TurboTax.

"U" is for

Universal health care.

It's high on Obama's list.
But Republicans say this means
That he is a Socialist!"

The United States spends far more per person on health care, about $4,500, than any other country, but U.S. life expectancy is 27th in the world. Forty-seven million Americans do not have health insurance. Obama pledged during his campaign to expand health coverage to the entire population, as many advanced nations already do. But as Hillary Clinton learned when she tried to enact universal health coverage 15 years ago, it's difficult to fight accusations of "socialized medicine."

"V" is for

VAMPIRE,

Rod Blagojevich, full of tricks.
He sucked from his victims their money,
The lifeblood of politics.

After the 2008 presidential election, **ILLINOIS GOVERNOR** Rod Blagojevich was caught on a wiretap trying to sell Barack Obama's Senate seat. The profane "Blago" called the spot "a [expletive] valuable thing—you just don't give it away for nothing." He was impeached, removed from office, and is facing federal corruption charges. But before he was kicked out, he used his powers to appoint to the Senate Roland Burris, a former Illinois state official who, it later emerged, had offered to raise money for Blagojevich.

"**W**" is for the politician's *Wife,*
Pushed into the public glare
When he asks her to stand at his side
As he announces he's had an affair.

Wronged wives (husbands haven't had it quite so bad) have gained new prominence in politics. Senator David Vitter, a Louisiana Republican, brought his wife on stage after his phone number appeared in the records of the D.C. Madam. Governor Eliot Spitzer of New York, a Democrat, did the same when he was caught visiting a prostitute. Senator Larry Craig, an Idaho Republican, took his wife along to face the cameras after he pleaded guilty to bad behavior in a men's restroom. But Jenny Sanford won applause for refusing to stand with her husband, Republican Governor Mark Sanford of South Carolina, when he admitted his affair.

"X" is in **FOX,** Rupert Murdoch's TV station.
Foes say splitting it from Republicans
Would require an operation.

"Fair and balanced" is the slogan, but with a lineup of conservative hosts such as Glenn Beck, Bill O'Reilly, and Sean Hannity, Fox News frequently draws the complaint that it is the house organ of the GOP. Republican lawmakers give the cable news channel preferential treatment, while Democrats denounce it. But imitation is the sincerest form of flattery, and MSNBC has turned itself into a mirror image of Fox News for left-wing viewers.

"Y" is for

YELLOW DOG,

A Democrat through and through.

Neglected by the party for so long,

Some say they haved turned blue.

A century ago, 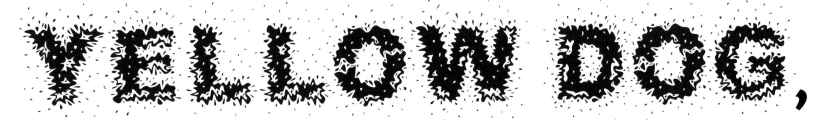SOUTHERNERS were so loyal to the Democratic Party that, the saying went, they would sooner vote for a yellow dog than a Republican. But in recent decades, the South went Republican (just as the Northeast went solidly Democratic), and many of the surviving Democrats from the South have joined other moderate and conservative Democrats from across the country to form the "Blue Dogs." The Blue Dogs, who number more than 50 in the House, like to describe themselves as yellow dogs who have been choked until they turned blue.

Z Z Z z

"Z" is for
The sound of the electorate's repose.
To get away with shenanigans,
Politicians need voters who doze.

ONLY 56.8 percent of voting-age Americans
showed up at the polls in 2008—and that was the highest turnout in years. In a typical presidential election,
barely more than half of eligible voters cast ballots, and turnout is downright dismal in the off-year
congressional contests: thirty-seven percent in 2006 and 2002. Many of those in the non-voting 63 percent
don't like what their government is doing— but they have nobody to blame but themselves.

THE END

Purchase high quality 18" x 24" posters of your favorite politicians at:

This book is available in quantity at special discounts for your group or organization. For further information, contact:

Triumph Books
542 South Dearborn Street
Suite 750
Chicago, Illinois 60605
312. 939. 3330
Fax 312. 663. 3557
www.triumphbooks.com

Printed in China
ISBN 978–1–60078–319-7

Book Editor: Mary Hadar
Copy Editor: Carrie Camillo

Illustrated and designed by Mark Anderson
Special thanks to Brian Anderson, Rob Brookman, John Beisty, and Anne Taylor Anderson for their help in developing selected illustration concepts.